P9-DYP-701

MIGHTY MACHINES

School Buses

by Kay Manolis

BLASTOFF! READERS

BELLWETHER MEDIA • MINNEAPOLIS, MN

Note to Librarians, Teachers, and Parents:

Blastoff! Readers are carefully developed by literacy experts and combine standards-based content with developmentally appropriate text.

Level 1 provides the most support through repetition of high-frequency words, light text, predictable sentence patterns, and strong visual support.

Level 2 offers early readers a bit more challenge through varied simple sentences, increased text load, and less repetition of high-frequency words.

Level 3 advances early-fluent readers toward fluency through increased text and concept load, less reliance on visuals, longer sentences, and more literary language.

Level 4 builds reading stamina by providing more text per page, increased use of punctuation, greater variation in sentence patterns, and increasingly challenging vocabulary.

Level 5 encourages children to move from "learning to read" to "reading to learn" by providing even more text, varied writing styles, and less familiar topics.

Whichever book is right for your reader, Blastoff! Readers are the perfect books to build confidence and encourage a love of reading that will last a lifetime!

This edition first published in 2009 by Bellwether Media.

No part of this publication may be reproduced in whole or in part without written permission of the publisher. For information regarding permission, write to Bellwether Media Inc., Attention: Permissions Department, Post Office Box 19349, Minneapolis, MN 55419.

Library of Congress Cataloging-in-Publication Data
Manolis, Kay.
School buses / by Kay Manolis.
p. cm. – (Blastoff! readers. Mighty machines)
Includes bibliographical references and index.
Summary: "Simple text and full color photographs introduce young readers to school buses. Intended for students in kindergarten through third grade"–Provided by publisher.
ISBN-13: 978-1-60014-180-5 (hardcover : alk. paper)
ISBN-10: 1-60014-180-3 (hardcover : alk. paper)
1. School buses–Juvenile literature. 2. School children–Transportation–Juvenile literature. I. Title.

TL232.M2838 2009
629.222'33–dc22 2008012232

Text copyright © 2009 by Bellwether Media Inc. BLASTOFF! READERS, TORQUE, and associated logos are trademarks and/or registered trademarks of Bellwether Media Inc.

SCHOLASTIC, CHILDREN'S PRESS, and associated logos are trademarks and/or registered trademarks of Scholastic Inc. Printed in the United States of America.

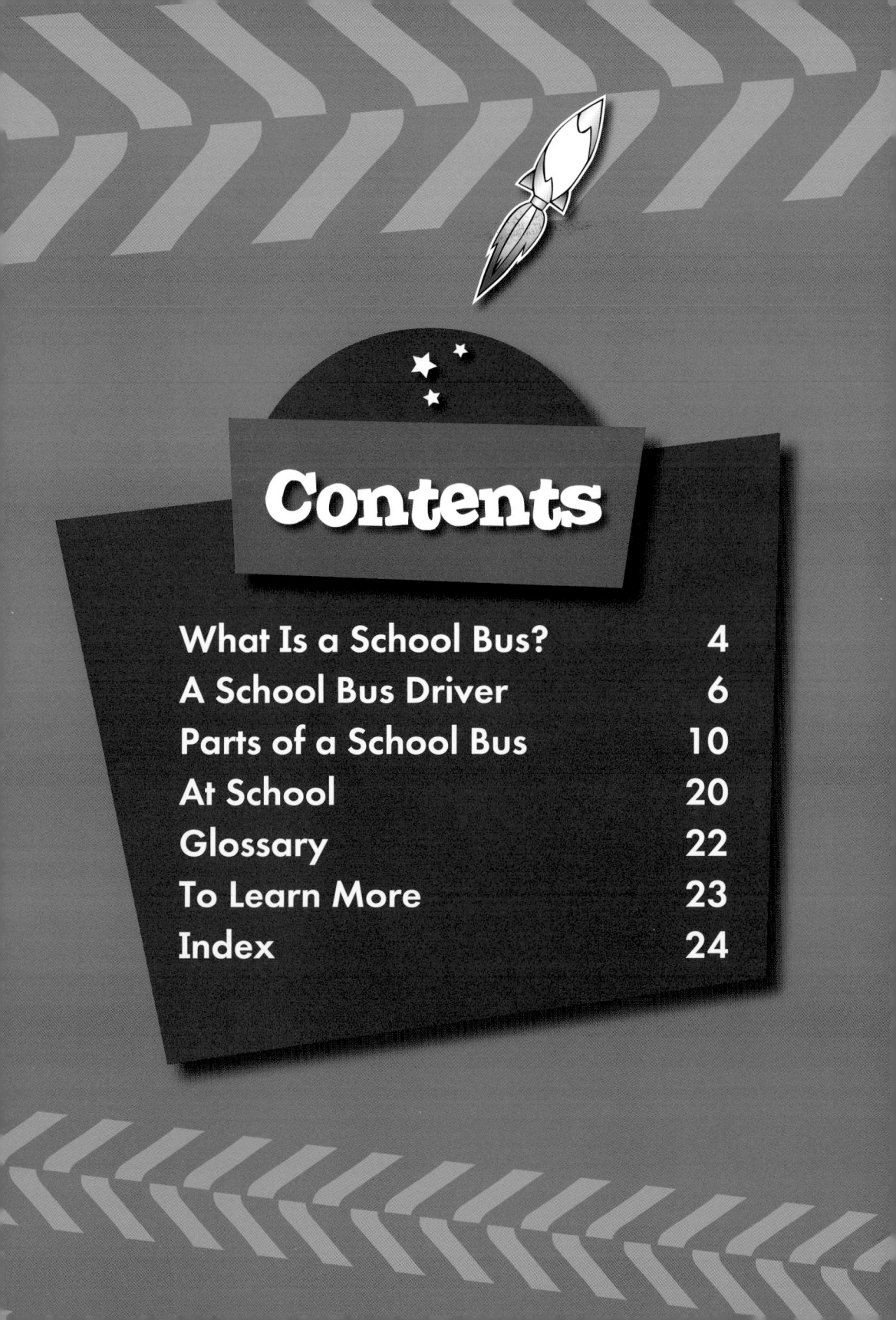

Contents

What Is a School Bus? 4
A School Bus Driver 6
Parts of a School Bus 10
At School 20
Glossary 22
To Learn More 23
Index 24

A school bus is a big machine. It can bring students to and from school.

34
USDOT 354406
GVWR 27,500
RESERVED

A school bus has a driver.

030269
THE RECOMMENDED MINIMUM TIRE AIR
PRESSURE FOR THIS POWER VEHICLE IS:
STEER AXLE
DRIVE AXLE (S)
PSI
PSI

The driver opens the door for students.

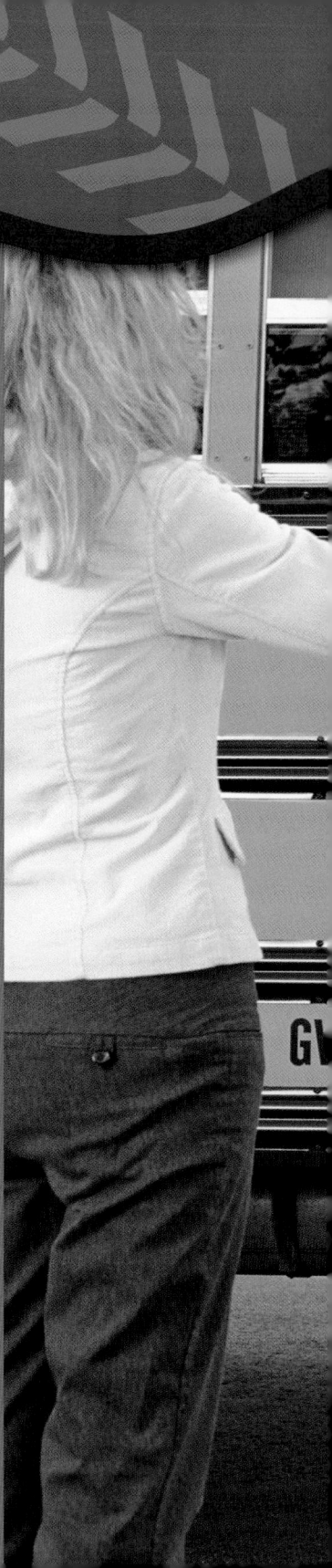

DO NOT DRINK
OR EAT ON THE
BUS!!!
030269
34
R 27,500

A school bus has red lights. These flash when the door is open.

SCHOOL BUS
EMERGENCY DOOR
STOP
STATE LAW

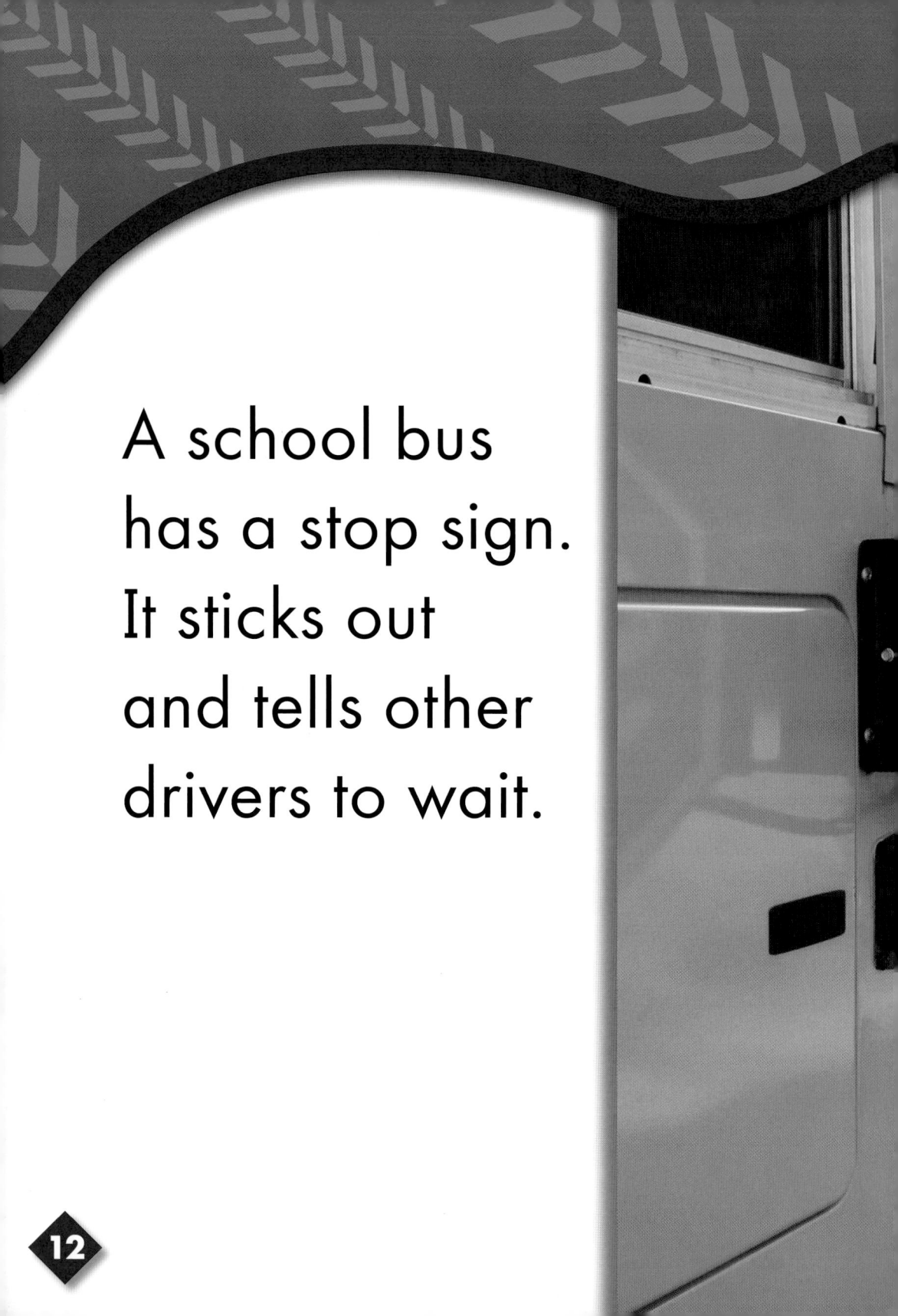

A school bus has a stop sign. It sticks out and tells other drivers to wait.

STOP

A school bus has an **aisle**. The aisle runs between the seats.

Some buses have a **wheelchair lift**. It can lift students into the bus.

UR STEP

School buses have an **emergency** door. Students can leave through this door in an emergency.

SCHOOL BUS
EMERGENCY EXIT
STATE LAW STOP
WHILE BUS IS
LOADING & UNLOADING
57

School buses drop students off at school. Have fun!

OL BUS

Glossary

aisle—an area between seats where people can walk

emergency—a serious problem or time of danger

wheelchair lift—a tool used to raise a wheelchair into a vehicle

To Learn More

AT THE LIBRARY

Crews, Donald. *School Bus.* New York: Greenwillow Books, 1984.

Feldman, Heather. *My School Bus; A Book About School Bus Safety.* New York: Rosen, 2000.

Zuehlke, Jeffrey. *Buses.* Minneapolis, Minn.: Lerner, 2005.

ON THE WEB

Learning more about mighty machines is as easy as 1, 2, 3.

1. Go to www.factsurfer.com
2. Enter "mighty machines" into search box.
3. Click the "Surf" button and you will see a list of related web sites.

With factsurfer.com, finding more information is just a click away.

Index

aisle, 14
door, 8, 10, 18
driver, 6, 8
emergency, 18
emergency door, 18
lights, 10
school, 4, 20
seats, 14
stop sign, 12
students, 4, 8, 16, 18, 20
wheelchair lift, 16

The images in this book are reproduced through the courtesy of: Nancy Louie, front cover; Matt Henry Gunther / Getty Images, pp. 5, 7, 9; Sonyae, pp. 11, 21; Jerry Horbert, p. 13; Rick Hinson, p. 15; Dennis MacDonald / age fotostock, p. 17; Carlos E. Santa Maria, p. 19.